Princess Rose

Princess Melody

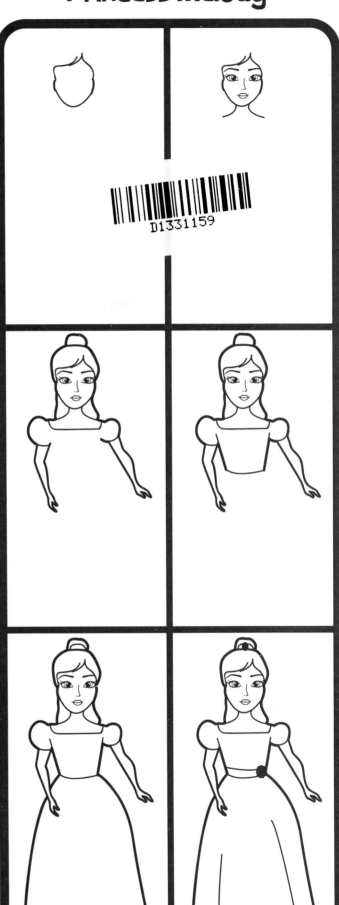

Princess Harmony

Princess Millie

Princess Baggage

Princess Yacht

Princess Hand Mirror

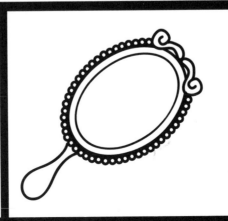

Princess Tiara

Princess Palace

Princess Sceptre

Crown Jewels

Princess Beach House

Princess Perfume

Princess Snow White

Princess Cinderella

Fairy Princess

Princess Aurora

Princess Party Cakes

Princess and the Frog

Princess Sunshine   Princess Willow

Princess Poodle

Royal Gardens

Princess Pony

Princess Dragon

Snow Princess

Arabian Princess

Wicked Stepsister

Princess Handmaiden

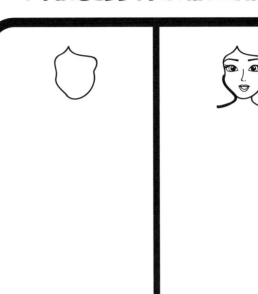
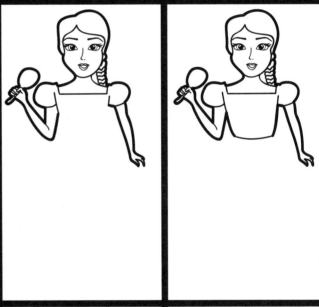

Thumbelina

Unicorn

Prince Charming

Princess Curtsy

Princess Playing Harp

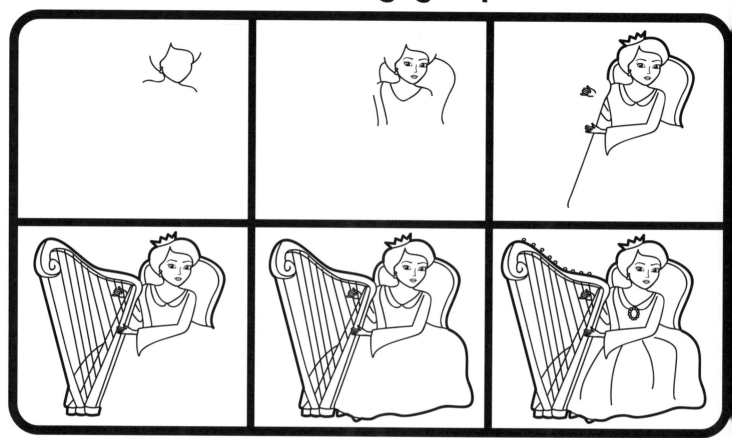

Princess at Spinning Wheel

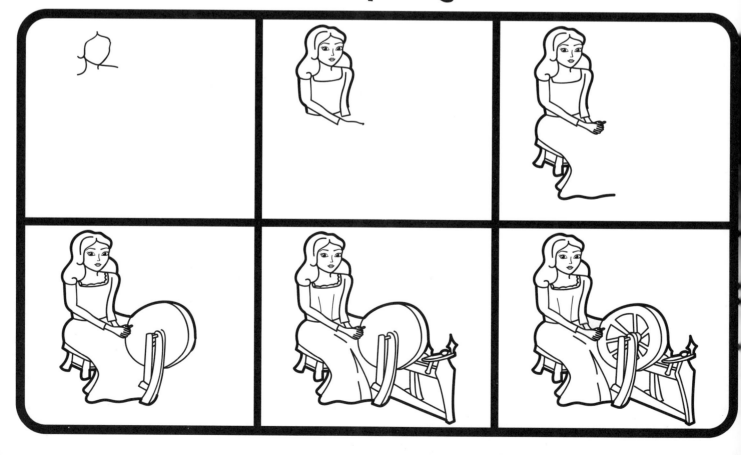

Princess Belle

Dancing Princess

Princess Sewing

Elf Princess

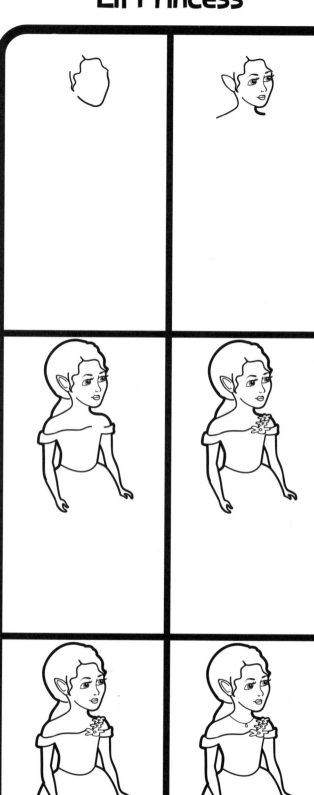

Princess Raindrop

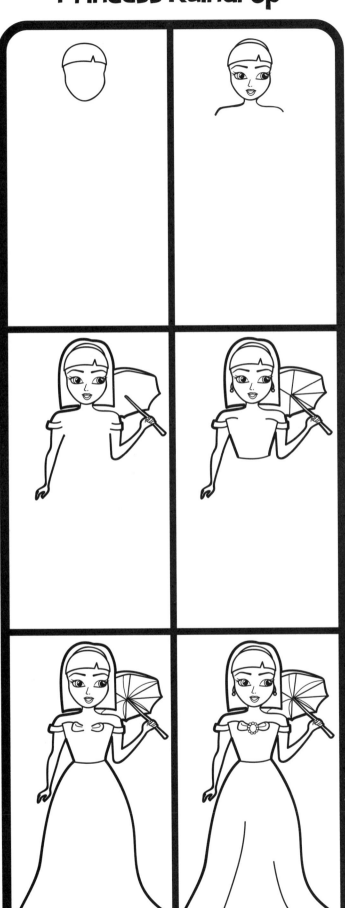

Queen

King   # Prince

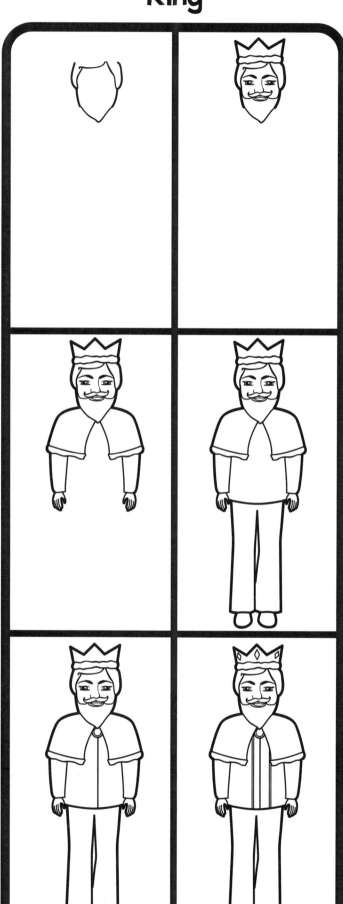

Royal Guard

Princess Birthday Cake

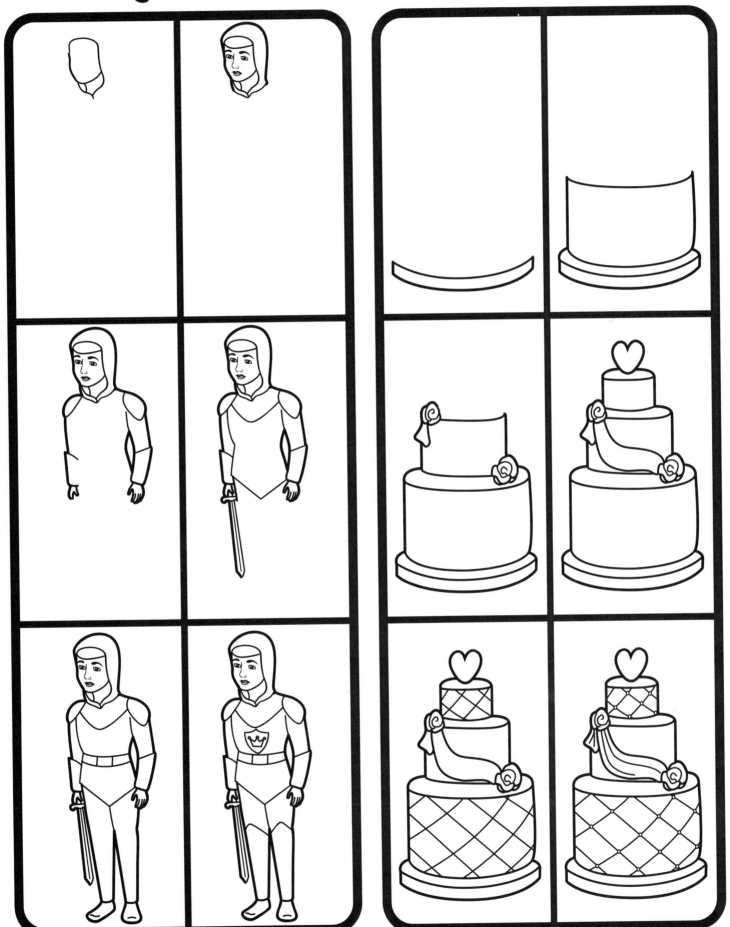

Egyptian Princess

Princess Oceania

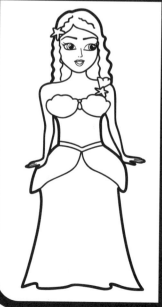

Angry Princess

Chinese Princess

Baby Princess

Princess Fencing

Princess Alexia

Princess Jasmine

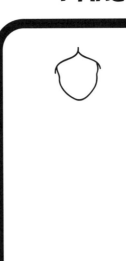

Indian Princess

Princess Amber

Princess Riding Horse

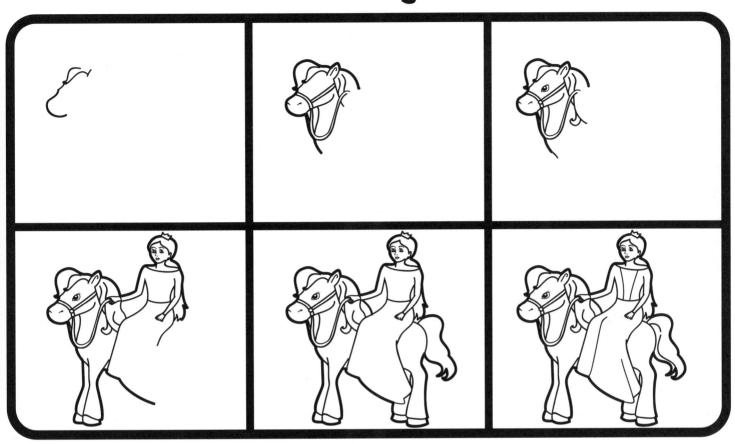

Princess Car

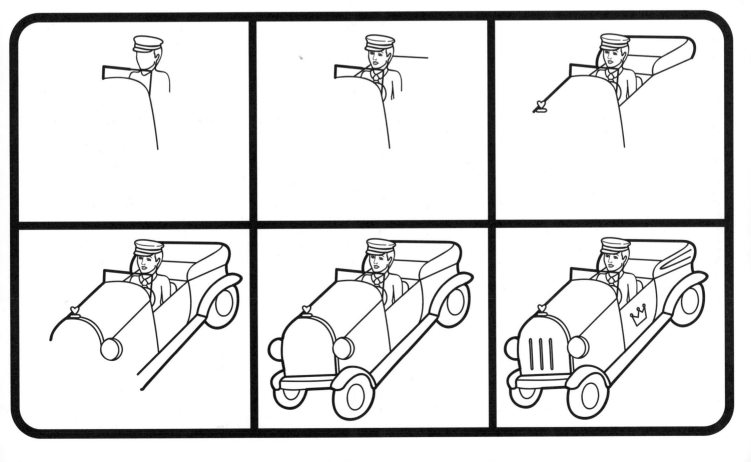

Princess Isadora

Amazonian Princess

Warrior Princess

Princess Isis

Wicked Stepmother

Alien Princess

Princess Sparkle

Pirate Princess

Princess Portrait

Sweet Treats

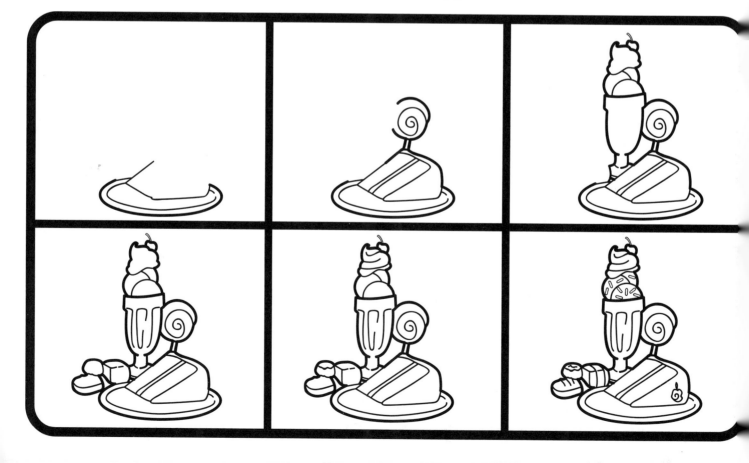

Princess Archer

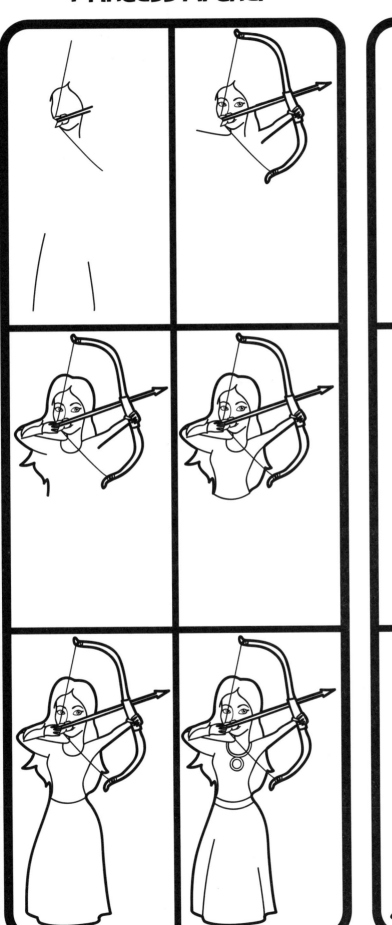

Princess Arabella

Princess Tulip

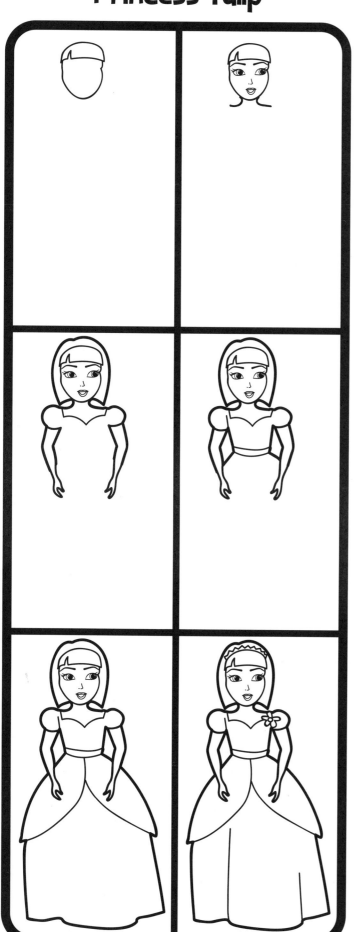

Princess Bethany

Princess Waving   # Princess Tiger Lily

Princess Arcadia

Princess Araminta

Princess and the Pea

Princess Tilly

Mermaid Princess

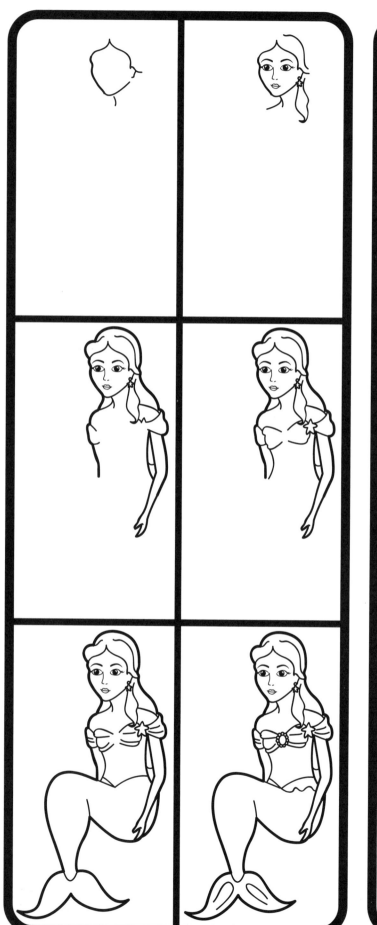

Princess Anastasia

Cheeky Princess

Princess Ellie

Princess Grace

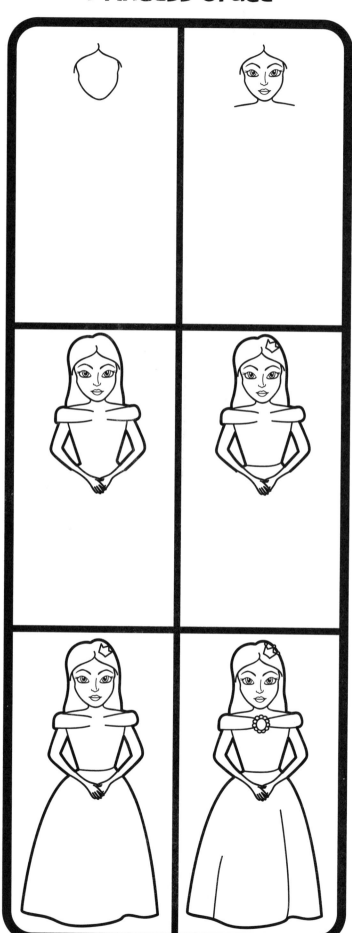

Princess Amita

Princess Katie

Princess Josephine

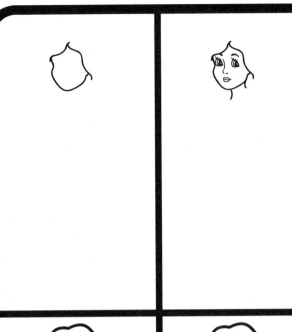

Princess Crown

Princess Carriage

Princess Tiara

Medieval Princess

Princess Lorna

Princess Dora

Princess Louise

Shoes fit for a Princess

Princess Island

Princess Hand Mirror

Prince In Love

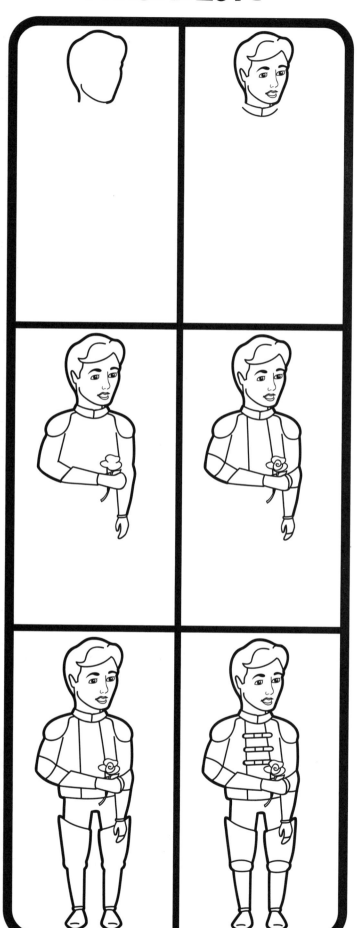

Princess Kattia

Princess Kathryn

Princess Carrie

Princess Bride

Princess Polyanna